BUENOS AIRES AND THE ORIGINS OF SAUSSE

AN ANTHOLOGY OF POETRY

by

Mel Vil

© Copyright Mel Vil 2014
Published by E. M. Crisp 2014
All artwork by E. M. Crisp

This book is sold subject to the condition that it shall not, by way of trade or otherwise, be lent, resold, hired out, or otherwise circulated without the publisher's prior consent in any digital or physical form other than that in which it is published and without a similar condition including this condition being imposed on the subsequent publisher.

First published in Switzerland in 2014 by E. M. Crisp

villemel.com

ISBN: 978-2-9545125-8-7

*To the city that does not attract me
and to Jorge,
who felt the same
and who is now here with me
in Geneva*

Table of Contents

Part I: Buenos Aires 7

The City Has Me (The Beginning) 9
The City Calling 10
Café Characters 11
The Girl 17
Buenos Aires Hustler I 19
Buenos Aires Dealer 22
Café Characters II 23
San Telmo 27
The Siesta 29
Being Alone 33
Most Out There 34
Border Run 37
Return to Buenos Aires 39
Buenos Aires Hustler II 44
Café Characters III 45
Argentine Queen 46
The Girl II 47
Night Walkers 48
The Addict 50
La Potota 52
Jardín Botánico (Botanical Gardens) 53
Will She Survive? 55
The Pampa (Lonely, Night Road) 56
Night Time 58
Thrown from Buenos Aires 59
Get Out 61

Part II: Bolivia 64

Sleeping Red Dragon 66
Inner Red Dragon 69
Shade (Midday Plus One) 72

Part III: The Origins of Sausse 74

Sausse Origins 76

Part I: Buenos Aires

The City Has Me (The Beginning)

The city has me,
I can't let go.
I want all its sins. Now.
Joda, droga, fiesta. All of it.
La que sea.
Noise, gossip, drugs,
Bright lights and brighter lies.

The city of whatever,
La cuidad de cualquiera.
I don't want it, but I can't leave.
If I leave I'll want it.
Its availability is indirectly
proportionate to my desire for it.

I like the idea of charging up,
Take you by the arm
Hit the street, talk a lot of shit.
Maybe dance, set some city parts alight.
Red. Some wine and love.
Together again.

The City Calling

Speak to me with strange sounds.
I don't understand really
Is the city communicating?
Crunch of stones underfoot
Jingled keys
Fumes being emitted
Engines revolving
Horns,
Brakes.

Are these the sounds of the city
Or do I have to decipher from the silences.
Silence's absence means nothing
The silent silence speaks
Doesn't care much for small talk
Worse, hates to be interrupted
Has left

Left the cats in charge
Too noisy, replace silence with cats,
Litter the park with kittens,
Come back when the noise has gone.
Let the cats sort it out, if they can.
What kind of cat doesn't boast.
What kind of park doesn't boast silence?

Café Characters

What makes a man
Use napkins to eat croissants?
I can't change this, I can only wait.
Watch from inside the window.
Wax my board, look for signs.
The threat of having sat
At some *viejo*'s table,
Is biting away
At the back of my mind.
They always cause a fuss,
Then refuse their table.
Get here earlier!
I have people to watch.

Here comes the rain again.
Falling on my head like a memory.
Here comes a black and gold
With its nose sagging.
Here comes a group of kids
Running for no reason.
Here comes a woman
Hugging a ¼ litre of clear liquor.

Now a undercover cop
Having a conversation
From a slow moving 70's Ford,

Pulling a pedestrian
Around the corner by a handshake,
They split,
The cop has to use his free hand
To help the window's mechanism.
A waiter returns a tray of dirty cups,
From some antique dealer,
No doubt.

A bus full of soldiers,
Eyes wide open.
Provincial youngsters
Treated to the corners of San Telmo.
Tourists stand out, different skin,
Different clothes.
Looks of bewilderment,
Perhaps.
Maps, bottled water,
Cameras and hats.
All the clues are there
If you have to look closely.
I see a lot of cheap clothing
Not the older generation,
Still wearing the same clothes
Bought twenty years ago,
Back when there were decent clothes.
Today's generation forty
Can't get out of denim and plastic.

How well do these people know each other,

It seems like café face recognition.
What of their real lives?
Do they talk about them?
It seems so unlikely,
You would expect gossip in a café.
An educated population,
This is utopia.
If only it wasn't a drug store.
A quick fix of espresso.
Not quite a fashion any more
Seasonal colour blindness,
The big give away.
So, coffee is the new black.

Where is that side of me today?
I need strength and confidence.
Which is my drug of need?
Which of these insipid vices is it,
That isn't working?
Where is the decisive vocal combination?
It'll come if it comes out.
There is a voice to accompany it,
A strong voice.
It tells people what I am going to do,
Or rather it lets them know,
For all I care.
The old guy leaves,
A writer by my estimate.
The black and golds get so close
At the crossroads.

To the point of nearly touching,
As the other rolls slowly by.
No one complaining,
Just the way it is,
No pasa nada.
The rules are your own,
The world is just overlap.
Here comes a change in the fabric.

Why is it possible to spot a man
Who lives a very basic existence?
Perhaps in the back of a van
Or some deserted warehouse.
Or even in the street.
You won't see him much,
But he'll be cleaned up when you do.
He has thin legs and a voluminous torso.
Swabby black, grey locks.
Scissor trimmed beard.
Today, a clean leather jacket.
He is in his street disguise.
Shape shifting for whatever necessity
Having brought him to our world.

A soaking-wet girl gives up
And stops a black and gold.
She throws herself against the seat
Almost violently.
Then lifts her head
And delivers the address.

A place, no doubt, warm and dry
I wonder if Roxanne had a roman nose
Or such black hair.
Not a blonde in a red dress, then?
Two uniform cops finish their break,
And get up to leave
As they reach the bar,
The owner reaches into the kitchen,
And passes them their jackets.

Multiple telephones start ringing
Eliciting varied response times.
All precalculated of course
Appearances really are that important
Interested in nothing except *quien hinchas*?

Café politics I suppose.
For me it's a second home.
My area of 'populated solitude'.
Where there are people,
Life and events.
Things I can pluck
From the air to play with.
But what are the chances
Of concentrating in such an environment?
It seems to be animate,
Always changing.
I need to be in solid situations.
I am emotionally diurnal.
But Today's a lazy Thursday,

Busy digesting last night's beef.
You can't pay to eat in a place like that,
But nothing beats your company, sweet thing.

The Girl

Quiet, dirt-avenued, provincial girl,
Southern apple sour to six degrees
Couldn't have picked a girl more like the city,
Or a city more like the girl.
Disease over patience
She made me do something I didn't want to do,
I am left very agitated.
Not a choice
Not a goal

When opportunity comes, I take it,
I should have done it a lot differently.
Should have taken the opportunity
To let opportunity to leave.
Should have left her
On one of her street corners,
Should have picked cocaine.
The future fiction is better,
Just let the time roll.
Over and over.
Now it is time,
To take this man on his journey,
Through his own mind.
Her words become a meditation,
To hypnotise was,
If not the whole reason,

Merely the coincidental result.
We are not the same,
Just interdependent.

Buenos Aires Hustler I

A man struggles
To restabilise his own personality
Not the type to sleep
Where he can to afford to live.
Each day a good day for him
In the *Good Air*,
A clean shower
Enough to make it perfect.
Like life on any street,
Not a hustle
Not a robbery,
But far from honest.
Never did a yoga class.
Sort of type to break
Into a quick step.
Smart and with it,
A gentleman and a scholar
Of the Discovery Channel
Never one to put his feet in footprints.

Not the guy who never falls,
This guy, you'll see him:
On a bus one day,
Drugged up and partied out,
Black around his eyes,
The oily reflection of his addiction.

It'll look strange,
To see him like that.
But you'll never see it twice in a row.
He keeps his money in two piles,
That's why.
Work and play,
When one runs out,
The party pauses.
Not one used to leaving
A night club broke and penniless.
That was his last bus
Trip back from a party.
Now he'll cleanse and rest,
Then eat and sleep
Get back on his feet,
Get back in the day game.
Build that second pile back up,
Wait for opportunity.
A smooth operator
Cutting fine white lines
With tiger's claws.

Escape one life of rules
And rule breaking for another,
Escape loan sharks wherever he can
Never losing the good spirit.
No contracts to tie him down
Free of strings and attachments
Ready to fly away now,
Get back home,

Make a new plan.
Go out and do it.
Live another five lifetimes
In several heartbeats
Then he'll throw a party
And treat people to a good time,
Playing the streets hard
And bringing the reward inside.

You can't keep a guy like this down,
You wouldn't want to.
Standing in front of shadowy doorways,
sunlight punching his silhouette
On the wall behind him.
Like some kind of superhero symbol,
His profile stands out,
His personality soaks into the environment,
He pulls at its energy using it for balances.
Riding the energy that's available,
Always fitting in,
Never having to do anything to ensure it.
Like a chameleon, shapeshifter,
Fitting the expectations of the people he meets.
Always the guy you are looking for.

Buenos Aires Dealer

Jesus is a hippy wannabe drug dealer, dancing with his arms to the heavens, his pockets full of pills.

He danced like a seductive anti-cupid in front of the mirror in the room today, like smoke, he is a phantom wisp above the cobbled streets of *San Telmo*,

His evil twin brother explodes into existence during a cloud burst of dust, heading off immediately to Caix and Pacha to pay the bills of kindness his smoky brother creates in his real world reincarnation.

Jesus is alive here in my little world, he pushes pills and disrespects entire neighbourhoods in swooping statements.

He floats in and out, from side to side tugging harder and harder on the good fabric, the good air.

There are doubts as to how strong the fabric is, it appears to be warping in his presence.

Will it hold or will it rip and suck him underneath, can he get out in time.

Or is he destined to be consumed?

Café Characters II

This city amazes me.
A private ambulance,
Followed by,
Municipal emergency vehicle.
Private bus,
Followed by,
Private taxis.

I'm sure somewhere
I've seen official street cleaners,
But I am never sure,
Who is paying them.
Beside, they get beaten
To most trash anyway,
If not *cartoneros*,
Then dogs or pigeons.
Whoever it is,
There is always someone cleaning.

Merchants wander in here all day
Hawking their products.
The run of the mill neighbourhood.
Most of this stuff just arrives.
Regular order:
Daily, weekly and monthly.
Oranges, meat, biscuits, bread.

The kids have poured out
Into the midday street.
Still a bleak day
But their noise and colour
Adds a little vibrancy to it all.
Life's persistent beat perhaps.
We are alive!
It hasn't stopped yet,
We can rejoice, at last.

Here is a stark image,
A young female.
Sports cap with neat leather trim.
Hair straightened and clean.
How to describe that jacket?
Nylon shell,
Three-quarter length,
Tailored to the waist
Foam insulated.
Murky turquoise.
She looks good
But it's still a parka,
And fashion by numbers.
She's not going anywhere,
But looking good going.
For her, at least,
It seems enough.

Six pigeons have the time of their lives.
The oligopoly on a pile of grain,

A large pile at that.
Undoubtedly more food
Than they've eaten
Between them,
All their lives!
Like some of us,
They have no idea how to stop.

A little girl's balloon
Rolls down the street,
Five minutes have passed
Since she danced by,
Bouncing happily.

A dog on a leash
Scares away the pigeons.
Only five come back.
The last sees its fate retires.

The streets are too wet and oily
To burst the balloon
Its misery will continue.
Like some of us,
Its quick exit from this world
Is not due
It will be alone for some time more.
Perhaps a taxi will take its life.
Will we hear its death cry?
If you see a tree fall,
But hear nothing,

Did it really fall?

And what would you want to hear,
If not the stories of me and my friends?
What this guy said to his wife last night?
We've had enough real life,
Let's discuss sex, rock and roll
Living, more sex,
Drugs and house music.
Why I want this girl,
What her assets are.
They come up short
Compared to the queen argentine.

This place is sublime,
It's out of control.
Some people come here
Just to lose control.
An inspiration for the hedonist.
Purely out of control.

Perhaps some older kid
Will stand on the balloon.

San Telmo

A paradise.
All things that do flow,
My ass do surf,
My dear serf.

What an ideal thing to say,
We have no foundations here.
We can let the ideas take over,
Too many tall, breasted,
Flowing haired girls.
Only girls with such nice hair,
Such nice bodies.
Too much coincidence.
Too slow the music.

It is irritating good music,
Just not to dance too,
Why don't they play the entire song?
We all have a great time,
Pinching your tits,
I just made it up,
So funny, the fear of him
And Liss Black.

That would have been a good show to go to,
Life just fills up and down on this planet.

The drugs and the friends,
Favours and payback.
Let's all fly away.

The Siesta

Not a solitary thought or dream
Is alone in the midday's midnight.
Quiet silence's echo sounds
From the peeling walls.
Drowned out by the subtle
Drum of another land.
What stimulates the afternoon
's peace, the siesta.
The time to rest,
Lie and wait for it to finish.
For what?
The loneliness of an un-fillable hunger
Roams in the streets,
Passing from hope,
Dashing black grills
To graffittied grey shutters.

Key concepts
When trying to grab
Hold of a place:
The angle's perspective
Denies subjectivity.
An objective mind
's lie is another man
's truth.
Time decided

How fast it would go.

Life pegged its rhythm
To an unknown currency.
An entity with the reluctance
Of a penniless hitch-hiker.
We live now,
In time with the shudder of a molecule.
A particle's heartbeat,
Tempo of life,
Vibrations in the fabric.
A millisecond's heartbeat
Combines to produce everything.

Lonely in the afternoon
Stuck in the heart of the city,
The ancient words of artists,
Since passed on,
Stories cling to the side
Streets and walls
Like million year old dirt.
To be washed away
In a second's thought.
Mental tsunami.

Undesirability is undesirable,
Unconstitutionally drained.
Who would swap this
For another afternoon?
A grand opportunity

To take a chance to slide through.
Perhaps unnoticed,
Unconnected to life.
Disassociate.
Can I walk a Möbius strip
In this city?
Walking from one side,
In line with ants,
To the other,
And track the dirt,
That belies their soles.

But appearing unchanging,
To the other.
A black ant
Among blacks
Yet red inside.
Inescapable risks,
Each new side,
The old side,
Repeated ad infinitum.
Unchanging?
Impossible.
Time takes away
Every moment's immortality.
The death of a period,
How long does one second live?
What is its life average span?
What is the deviation?
The variance?

What is its opposite?
Anti-time?
Time machine?
The siesta, of course.
The period of time
Where things appear to go backwards.

Being Alone

Unwritten
(the antithesis of the untitled work, an unworked title)

Most Out There

Torrid fighting, I have to leave.
Stand up, try my best to look hurt.
Walk away,
Step by step.
The hot sand is burning my feet.
My soul, too crushed for running.

The board walk the way out,
It's not cool.
And there's a cloud burst.
A Pampa travelled storm.
hits the end of the road
The exodus begins. The beach drains.

I walk perpendicular to their screaming,
Drops fall, the air claps and flashes.
Captivating
The smell of rain on ocean.
It slips my mind I was *walking away*
I quicken my pace. I must get back.

The sand softens to warm and damp,
No longer do I skip
Over retained energy.
Drops fall faster.
The climax is a clap of thunder, I start.

Shocked into running as if struck by the bolt.

My unused, depleted, weak muscles twinge.
A wet slap to the system's face.
Gives me goose bumps.
All my senses detect change.
Wetter, darker, cooler, more solitary. All changing.
As each if footstep carved away another second of the day.

The town shrinks away.
The ocean remains as faithful as the sand.
Apartments become houses,
Become mansions.
Not everyone's view is spoilt,
By clubs or people. Expensive luxury built on cheap solitude.

I have run into another world. Not a soul exists.
The beach has become heady and bulky,
Sticking out,
Bullying the shrinking ocean.
Am I on top of the world? It is illusionous.
If anything I am just closer to the sky.

I reach the 'Most Out There' beach post.
A wooden refuge for withdrawing
Adrenalin junkies.
And lone runners
No more kids, dirt bikes, horses or romantic couples.

Just my body, the sky, water, sand and blue disks.

Blue disks, perpendicular to the sunset, like giant pills,
Sunk into the sand, by someone no doubt,
To contrast the sky.
Between purple-indigo north and Orange-terracotta west.
Above the sea, a green and turquoise reflection fades into
Patagonian greys, whites and blacks. Full circle.

I have to stop. Stop to look around.
Everything that was, has disappeared.
Even the rain has stopped.
A little further lies somewhere else,
A million miles from where I didn't want to be
Free from bonds and feeling, out there.

Border Run

A long journey has no words, I can't speak.
I feel the energy,
I feel the need to be reenergized.
By the forces of a mountainous retreat.
In a stark dry valley with an orange sunrise
Through blonde, stalky grass bushes.
Stark contrasts.

Twenty minutes before the sun rises.
Two thousand kilometres
To spend these twenty minutes, lost.
Standing still.
Twenty minutes,
Standing still,
Being cold.
Standing cold,
Still and examining my thoughts.
Counting stars,
Counting journeys.
Counting kilometres of life.

When will I stop,
Or is it the world's decision
To stop rotating.
Leave us spinning
Stationary with stationery.

Inspired to live
Inspired to stop living.
Stop living it up.

Travelled or not,
Welcomed or stopped.
No more.
Not to Bolivia,
At least.
Each trip becomes shorter.
Each mouthful more cautious,
Likewise with breathing.

Perhaps in my own transport,
To avoid some of those perils,
There was a reason to come initially
It is in these words:

Dry, dry valley
Existing in my memory,
Blazing contrasts,
To form parts of my 'self',
Red mountains how you tame
My deep, blue sky.

Return to Buenos Aires

Back in Buenos Aires,
I come back often, it seems.
This time it's good
That it's become somewhere familiar.
And that I am at a clean table,
Good coffee on its way
More confidence, more Spanish.
Safer, like being at home.

Latin American capital after other.
Neither could they be
Nor will even one,
Be anything like it,
Take the cafés.
By way of example.
A home from home.
A respite from the outside chill.

From the streets I love to roam
I have fallen.
Aimlessly, but not without objectives
Of unknown certainty
To an unknown priority, hungry.
The streets I like to roam
Always in search of that perfect place to stop.
To fall and collapse,

To soak the warm sun.

Away from the cold street,
Through the medium of glass barriers
Separating stained white foam and pastry
From biting breeze and smoking exhaust.
Protection and safety have been found.

Once found, harmony returns.
The chatter of *porteños*
The gurgling coffee machines.
Indoor plants and 24 hour news.
Contrasting temperatures.
Veritable greenhouse.

From my careful ledge
I see the world fly.
Shiny black-and-gold cabs,
Newspaper headlines in kiosks
Street vendor dancing by
With dainty steps over potholes,
Where drain covers should lie.

Twelve degrees, it says.
I feel tropical sunshine.
Through the plants and glass
Funny, cold and heated inside.
Yet also cold and heated outside.

The traffic surges red hot.

Avenues pulsate with people.
Fighting to get their first.
Making the city seethe.

Inner city service stations dwell,
Dwarfed by modern apartment blocks.
Ridiculed in turn by colonial beauty
Although injured.
Architectural injustices advance.
Take a closer examination.

Has that wall and buttress been destroyed?
Has this historical monument,
Protected in most lands,
Been violated?
Pockmarked with air conditioning?

Badly torn hole,
You shabby stain on the wall
Filled with loosely fitting fridge.
At this time of year, it's a sight.
Injustice unjustifiable.

Tatty edges of apartments and private office
Meet at various angles of image.
Sharp and pressed straight edges.
Belonging to none other than
Bank and insurance companies.

Random coincidences

Creating mazes of contrasts
Repeating over and over
Block after block
The unit of labyrinth.

But I've noted well,
Here there is no misdirection
Nor indecision
All the creatures of the maze
Know their way around
Each and every route mapped out.
Each with a place to go.

A place to be
A child to take somewhere
A person to meet.
Something to pay or buy.
Nothing on a personal level
Could ever be that random.

No taxi drivers hailing
Or bus destinations screamed.
The continent's impulsiveness stops here.
No one stops their day
At the whip of a screamed city.

No keys waved,
Nor fingers pointed
Not a hand flapped
Telling people where they could go.

Don't try it
They don't like it.

The European availability of anonymity reigns.
And is available.
Even flyer touts have wound back
Accepting that perhaps we don't want
What they have.

There is no universal pressure here.
Except that which forces each self inside
Compressing it into a seething motivation
A city's silent instruction
Pressure to have purpose.

Pressure to know where you are going
To have a place or to have a purpose
To know what you want
To fit in and look pretty
A different style of pressure.
To handle pressure with style.

Buenos Aires Hustler II

The hustler has a brother,
But forget the speak of the other brothers.
They live abroad to export drugs home,
They live here living the life,
They live lying in graves and cells.
They can't all be accounted for,
They'll never be seen together,
In the same place
At the same time.
But they're around,
Wherever you go.
Sliding thirty grams a week
Without battering an eyelid.
No problems either.
They're big strong lads.
Several layers deep, too.
No flies on these guys.
Nice guy gets treated well.
Ladron steals from one of them,
They'll want to kill.
Think of the millions of miles
Further they would go
If they didn't have *pelo de concha*.

Café Characters III

The professor tutors his student,
Over a soft drink!
And a coffee, in a corner café.
Past the corner travels:
Black and gold taxis,
Pastel striped buses,
And their fumes.
Delivery boys,
On delivery bikes.
Waiters with trays
Covered to keep out the rain.
A teeming populace of artists,
Who circulate endlessly,
Ad infinitum.
Seemingly producing nothing,
Just wearing the paving,
Free of charge.

Argentine Queen

Please see Being Alone (above)

The Girl II

Another night of ecstasy,
I fell in love again.
I was just looking at her,
I told her I was a quiet person,
and having a quiet night.
I came here, to you, to dance.
Just a blonde child.
One night's infatuation.
I really came for the music.
Not the drug.
Describing what I feel inside is easier than telling you.
I think you are an objectively attractive person.
What lies, lies beneath.
It isn't time for change,
I need to change something for time,
I have no time to tell you I love you,
Loved up love duck.
Where do you want to go?
Who do we take with us?
What do we want to take away with us?
You want more,
I want more,
The lines of mutual exclusivity.
Time never comes, like tomorrow
never yields like yesterday.
and never feels like right now.

Night Walkers

Night time and still air.
Palermo to Retiro.
Different blocks,
Different people.
But all those forced to beat blocks.
Night walkers,
Late shifters,
Street shiners.
Polishing the *veradas*,
Length and breadth of *avenidas*.
Where arteries meet,
Worlds cross.
Set people side by side.
You have walkers
Walking from all walks of life.
Stepping down to the gritty truth
The down-town terminals.
Grotty and snotty,
Where night children eat.
Unslept and in a blaze
Not unlike me, tired.
All of us sat in oily, recirculated air.
A rest bite from the walking.
A break from the blocks.
Place to put the feet up,
Eat a *choripan*.

Wait for a bus or train.
Dissipate heat from the feet.
None of us live here,
But we are all from the same place.
A place that requires
More walking
To reach.
Always.

The Addict

An innocent man sits and waits
For his addiction to take over.
Waits for it to drag him and take him
On the ride he has been waiting for.
Waits for his own psyche to distract him
With his many other obsessions.
He is fraught with what he had
At one moment, then lost.
He is fraught with what he gave up
And fraught to have it back.
He toys with just how it'll be
If he'll be able to appreciate having it back.
Little does he know
Of what he has lined himself up for.
As little as he knows
Of the time left to get back up,
To find it
To grapple it,
To take him back.

Watch him as he leads his life
Dividing it into social sectors.
Decision made with each paradigm,
Rarely intersecting.
But as he pushes for the top of each circle,
His aura widens.

Societies overlap.
Soon everybody knows everything.
He tries to cut back,
To cool the heat.
He looks to subcontract,
But finds he is no longer trustworthy.

He has recently been haunted.
A voice was put inside his head.
Now it sets rules for him,
Like not eating in front of the poor.
He looks back at his consumptive periods
Vast quantities, little care
And much disregard.
Blind to the people around him.
He no longer defines himself
By his behaviour?
Something has really taken control.

La Potota

You have to go exploring sometime.
Summertime.
Find the place
Where early morning hides us.
Filters shattering rays
Through its wide glass expanses.
Over hot leather sofas
Fluctuating body temperatures.

Green glass dripping
Delivering sweat.
Obsessed by eyes for a while
Crystal blue meth in shades of smile.
In a thought, animals wander wild
Live trains of purple raindrops and style.
High quantities and low demand
Choke out lives

A daylight transaction
Over a black table is sly.
We see the stars
Light up our eyes
So come watch us entertain
The universe with our lies.

Jardín Botánico (Botanical Gardens)

A spoilt countenance loved lost
A gentle feline by my side
Cold grip on my face, side
This is the slow life
Passing perhaps in my favour
Who knows?
It's not too hard to not fight too hard.

It's a fresh smelling deserted castle.
Lovely house in wealthy surroundings.
This red floor's reminiscent
Of a climate suitable for us all
Alone with cats and green
Red and feline.
Pasa todo el mundo
every type
every reason
such is the city
sucking love from the country
leaving dry souls
Who's daily park visits,
Have to suffice.
Suffice to say it is enough.
The sun breaking
Over the red brick battlements.
Each to his own,

Englishman to his castle
Sunshine marking the difference.

Growth of a smile,
The leaves to our skin,
Site for chlorophyll breeding?
Take a vitamin pill instead
I don't like the tree standing,
It'd look much better horizontal,
Chopped and diced
Underneath a set of coffee cups
Made from imperial porcelain.
Perhaps some biscuits and doilies,
But definitely in the living room.
Can live with a tree
Under these conditions only.
Do we mind a road or two,
Or a reading table or two?

Here at least I own both contrasts.
A nice place for my nice coffee cups,
A few blocks walk and I get to feel alive,
The yellow shine on the red soil,
The glittering green and leafy yellow edges.
The trees and their shade, the balance.

Will She Survive?

I sit in cold and coming down,
On the *costanera*,
In front of *River Plate* stadium,
Being taught etiquette according to the PFA,
He deems they need no further instruction,
As to how to police young rapscallions,
They don't tell me how to write,
Or so they say,
Instead they teach me how to bribe.
Let's call it a tip.

They scare me even more now.
Knowing how unprovoked they are.
They're hungry,
That's all that's important.
Out of cash?
Best have a 'get out of jail' card
And to keep it handy.

Don't leave yourself stranded
Without that *plata*,
I know what I want,
My freedom,
Not another moment
Of cold, damp, grey to pass by.
And you? Money? Am I right?

The Pampa (Lonely, Night Road)

I love the feel of the wind and air
How it moves through you,
Instead of moving you.
Wind and air for a change,
Of a place that knows no change.

I love the night lights
The wideness of the *pampa*.
There is no need to waste money
Reaching for the sky,
When you have such vast open spaces.
The buildings are long slabs
Fallen obelisks.
Steam trains displayed
In front of factory entrances.

I love watching empty
Forecourts and parking lots
From the inside comfort,
Of an air-conditioned, overnight bus.
Row upon row of car shelter,
Protecting leather upholstery
Not from the moons powerful rays,
But managerial tempers
And so seem lonely and pointless,
Soldiers under lowered flags.

I love the complex traffic systems,
Distributing into the cities.
The sense of repetition, over and over.
They are complete and anonymous,
You could be anywhere,
On any one of them.

I love that all you can see at night
Is the belt of fallen stars
Separating where you are
From what is far away.
Leading my mind astray
To these broad, clear horizons?

I love the nothing.
Nowhere have I seen so much,
Unique in its basics,
Most places with nothing, have less.
But here you will find trees,
Scrub bushes and dirt.
Away from the roads, animals perhaps.
Yet small units,
And big measurements, mean
Repetition sets in again.

I love that the only thing that changes,
Is how you feel.

Night Time

Night time fallen, cold ears arrived.
But both fall on cold ears of those leaving
The silence falls more solidly in winter.
The rush is more smooth now.
A calm flow.
They're leaving, it sighs in quiet relief.

Now to rest, at least remove shoes
A hard day polishing the streets,
Working the cipher
Now it is time to enjoy the fruits,
The daily rewards.

Behind they leave the city,
With no place to go.
It will walk all night, walk until it passes out.
No choice between food, drink and smoke,
Or the love of a good woman.
Tonight, the city has no place to go.

Thrown from Buenos Aires

The crushed hopes
Of a conflicting love dope.
Unbelievable anger
In the face of romantic danger
Solutionless soul;
Bagged, tagged and unresolved.
A new future
No longer based on a life's past
Think of an exquisite description
For my uncertainty.
Don't let yourself be undermined
By my *bronca*
Thrown on a fire,
Burn bitch!
Life is out.
Control is a word of forecast,
Rain is due.
Like solid grey drops of water,
I stain

My entire life
The high preceding this low
My plain desire gone,
Ecstasy—my heart's substitute.
A lesson in love diplomacy,
Learning the hidden laws.

Understand better life's fabric,
Find lose threads.
From which it should be easy to unravel.
Perhaps it'll be a clear coast,
A port town to return to.
However, I can't make another attempt yet.
Now is the time of my departure,
I take my leave.
Returning with my heart
Between my legs,
Hoping the road will cleanse.

Get Out

Flows of magma and hatred
Roll villages into ashy graves
On the banks of our oceans.
I, on the other hand,
Am a particle
Being bounced
Around my own interior,
Pushed from one unbelievable situation,
To another,
Arriving at each,
Only to have my pleas for asylum,
Some form of refuge,
From social emotion and torture,
Rejected.

What are you telling me?
My own advice regurgitated,
And coming from my new surrogate.
It amounts to nothing. None. *Nada*.
All I know is,
Wherever I am,
I feel the need to leave.

I don't have time for anxiety
I am moving too fast,
I have control underneath,

Where it needs to be,
Superb perseverance.
Super cool exterior.
Need to keep desire
Out of my list of desires.
What I have to do to survive,
My principle aims:
Simplicity and focus.
Get away from my current,
Negatively charged,
Situation.

Part II: Bolivia

Sleeping Red Dragon

Sleeping red dragon,
Ancestor of who
Sleeps at high altitude
Escapes what?
Creating a dry Martian valley
Only suggestive of some phobia

Does dragon dread drowning
Afraid of deep blue puddles
Always referred to
How tall are you dragon?
Dare you tell?
Rock scales and leafy respiration
Springs of natural source, dragon tears.

These expansive plains,
Your doing?
Surely.
And to lift you from your slumber
Oh red wonder!
Clapping hands and,
Clopping hooves
Don't work
Nor the footsteps of man,
Woman or dinosaur either.
You have stories, too.

You could tell me your story
Of green envy
For having dragged me,
Once more.

How do your flames allow life
To grow in this inhospitable terrain
We're you fatally flawed
By some emerald eyed greed
How jaded are *your* eyes,
Sleeping red dragon
Hidden how deep,
Beneath these over-mined mountains,
Is your soul?
You draw me back again,
In search of answers.
You sleep,
Do I molest you?
Why invite me back
Stay friends all around,
Already roamed.
Through red hills and tearless rivers.
Your discourse of sleep,
Bores the fainthearted,
And awakens deep thinkers.

Your stash is gone,
Its new master soon after.
Even cowboys don't get far walking.
How precious is the real treasure.

What must I do to realise it
Or do I presume too much.
You need a guard
A real protector
For your hibernating season.

More than one gunfight
Took place here,
More than one reason
Brought you here,
You had the choice of the world.
You had infinite options,
But here you sleep,
Under my words.
Less than conversation.
Low frequency breathing
Seismic inquietude,
Your red arched back
In pretence of a rock.
There are real treasures
That shouldn't be mined
A few of us know you,
But you know us all

Which will find the truth?
I hope me.
I hope no one
I hope we are here for a reason,
Red dragon.

Inner Red Dragon

Red dragon, sleeping rock
Harsh cemetery, dry scales.
I can see your rocky ghost,
Burgundy back
Lifeless lizard,
Soothing sun.

I can't take our overseer's piercing ray,
Perhaps you can,
Perhaps you are just waiting,
Resting your soft white stomach
On the cool valley floor.
Drinking water from the river.

Somewhat shallow,
Call covering,
Tepid temperature
Where is your fire?
Based on precious metals
Yet stolen from within?
Coin de-operated.

What brings me back here?
To sit and write?
To tell stories of your scaly back
Bad ways and worse methods

Do you mock me?
What should I do with your rose inspiration?
Your tormenting treatment.
Your red back, unshifting.
Patiently blood warming
While we cower in leafy shade.

What of the cool breeze,
Fleeting through this valley,
Composed in part,
By one of your flanks
Chilling to a point.
Firing its way
Through our variety,
Of flaws and weak-points.
Neither your fiery breath
Nor your smoky trails

Can the poverty of your people
No longer fuel the fire
That used to burn inside
Have they ignorantly clipped
Your innocent wings
Will you fly once again?
Soaring above in the Andean aviary,
Will your power ever return?
Will you see another day?

For now I know nothing.
I watch you, climbing

To your neck in my mind.
Aiming for the white cross,
That religious dagger
Shallowly buried in your nape.

I fall to my knees,
Blank of oxygen and struggling,
From my vertical efforts,

I reach out, throwing my arms
Towards the cross,
Looking for support,
From its shoulders.

But it is weak,
Its basis is but basic.

It folds.

Its arms break off in mine.

Shade (Midday Plus One)

I cling to pink walls,
Praying for midday plus one,
When will the street be
Half covered with cool.
I hop, sandalled and hatted,
From alley to alley.
Side street to side street.
I seek high walls.
My feet are cold,
Yet my hair scorches.
I cling to pink walls,
Praying for midday plus one.

Part III: The Origins of Sausse

Sausse Origins

Thursday thudder, wasted and ill,
Drugged to the eyeballs,
At least the coughing has stopped,
Coke helps on that shit too.
Blank page, undistracted.
Lights are not off, but not bright.
Unidentified page.
The blankness.
Invention of illness.

The twisted convoluted irrealities
Of the sick's world.
How do we cope
With the lies and creativity
Of the overheated mind,
Boiled into a dream
Of the awake.
Sensory torture
Over the impossibility
Of what my senses
Are trying to tell me.
It's not real they cry.
This hallucination
Is not produced by a drug,
Just some unfortunate coincidence,
A cocktailesque combination

Of medication and recreation.
Hardcore emotional stress,
Makes me wonder,
How women make sense
Of anything,
When I get emotional
I just lose control.

Absolute hell.
A tough life.
Clockwork,
Women whose lives
Are only half consumed
By being irrational.
We need to start taking care
Of our serotonin levels,
We're hanging out
With a lot of crazy chicks.
The only thing I know
Is that it won't be level,
And I would much rather
That it be level.

Just the habit of writing.
My bisexual girlfriend
Used to write down stuff
In her little pocket notebook
All the time.
Crazy things,
She actually liked it,

She was interested
In my bullshit.
Muy loco.
As fucked up as she was
I still really loved her.
That's probably why
I loved her,
Because she was free, giving,
In the beginning at least,
She was selfish afterwards.
But she kept up with me,
We drunk and danced
And did things together.
She could keep up in conversations.
A really greedy person.
For a really long time
It was really great.

Bubbles, the creative process.
Like the little Josh diagrams,
Not the breast man,
Who turned me into a boob man.
How can you not be a breast man?
Six feet, giant lips, big blue eyes
And olive skin.
A domineering diva.
A big open invitation
To extract all the carnal pleasures
You have ever dreamed of.
She would bring home girls for me,

It was nice. At first.
Sinful. But nice.
It never felt sinful.
It feels like we both
Wanted to do something
Extravagant.
And it just happened to be
Something we both wanted
To experiment in.
When the third girl left,
We just came back together,
They were just like toys.
Kind of the same way an animal
Might only eat half its kill.
Talk about life
And what people have been through,
Their events.
Static noise in the signal of the planet,
Vibrating,
The life that exists
Gives of the same frequency?
So they say,
I hope,
I buzz,
In time with the liberated.
I don't want to get stranded
On the planet
While the positive vibrators
Lifted off to the next
Destined to host the living

Parasite that is nature.
The next environment
For her to send her worker bees
War horse, and honey ants
To establish another stock-market.
Same shit different planet,
Drained of its resources
Can't even label it good or bad
Just straight forward usage.
What is provided
By who ever created all this
Owner or ownerless.

Free or communal,
It's there why shouldn't we use it,
Just because afterwards
There will not be anything
Lying around,
Thinking about cartoon characters
With wide eyes and all this
Spread out,
A mouth like a goat

Very, very *especial*
Muuy muy bueno!
Very good cocaine!
People wrapping cocaine all their lives,
They can probably eyeball
Better than any scale.
But today I noticed some inconsistency,

Maybe a new person in the line.
The knots were big and fat,
On long strings,
Or perhaps they are outsourcing,
The cops might be in on it.
Always showing up to harass people
No reason or time
It's all big shit money fucked.

Call her back sends me an email,
Call her again,
She still hasn't called me back.
She's a man-eater.
I am a hunter.
I hunt women,
The crazier the better.
And sure, I get cuts and
Grazes along the way.
It's nature's *modusperandi*
The rules are there,
The invention too.
We use solitude.

Company.
The combination right now,
Plucks words from the matrix,
Fabricates a world of its own,
Perhaps one where nobody
Has a sense of taste
Or one where drinks

Have bubbles
In place of liquid,
And liquid
In place of bubbles.
Elsewhere,
Known as
The anti-*gaseosa*.
In this world,
It'd take hours to rehydrate,
Perhaps an overnight task.
But no beer.
A place where people slept upright
And wandered around all day
On electric beds
Like monopods

Why cant I get into something
Land a big fish and make a killing,
Sit back reeling ideally,
Call it the easy life
And not even explore my consciousness.
Or is this just idle
Is this just a ride?
I deal not in books
That no one cares about,
That exist a few hours apart
On a train to the beach
To stretch the limits
Of imagination and reality
To test people's nerve.

I drag you wherever I go
To take you with me
To not be alone.
To have a someone I came with
Not even just to have someone
To dress up and organise
But to have a purpose of being.
Here while I talk idly
About doing business
I'm never going to do.
Perhaps.

Motivation allowing,
A new drug is being pushed,
Feeding into a thriving party scene.
The welcomers and the opposed
Embrace and wrestle.
The components of the network
Rearrange.
The underground after party
Kings in the city of queens
And *ladrones.*
What a place to set a love story,
Or to set up a double cross
The unknown and unexplored
Side with the city,
Leading nothing nowhere,
But through crisis and protest
Murder and murder cases
The nonchalance of the dead,

Killed in shoot outs.
The obsession with tracking down
Murderers of the famous.
Here it is.
It's all inside
Just floating in the big ocean
Pick a direction and imagine,
Never doubt anything
What you're doing
Is not worth the time and effort
All experience is material.

You will see what ever you want,
And they will interpret it
Anyway they want.
That is what is laid out
Before you.
I predicted a place
Where people do not smoke.
I can call that significant,
And that this moment is then defining
By definition.
But whatever I do from here
Is the beginning of something bigger.
Every time to sit and think,
I allow myself to dig into the culture.
But always with an eye on the clock
Spend too long in
And become part of it.

The dangers of epicurean Argentina.
Sure, there is plenty enough,
But surplus will rot,
Prodigal son.
Leave and see new things
Dream them up, live them,
Then return
And enjoy the success
Don't be stranded
It's another small pond,
Limited circulation is possible.
Not necessarily bad for you
But think down the line,
Depending on how much
You allow the future,
To define yourself
If it was a large percentage of life
Then it is part of you,
Although this method,
Slurs us with its pimps
And bad X
The same as the *facu*
If I had stayed
It would have tarred me
I got in
Persevered throughout,
And then just when,
I thought I'd projected,
I found myself being ejected

Good fortune landed me here
And I now do the same
But something bigger,
Take something interesting
And make something out of it
Then say *adios*
See you later
Get to the next hot spot.
Instincts never failing,
Creating anything,
Meditating on change,
Considering crossing
The famous ocean of the *I-ching*

Then there's the morning pause,
Watermelon-seed coloured
Kentucky-fried Cosby kids
To be dropped off at the pool.
The dangers of Argentina
A green line
Fragment
Don't consider revising
Why want to revise
Being fragmented
By the capital of such a country?
Why can't we live
In a world where
Everyone just wants everyone else
To have a good time?
Let people fight,

Don't complain.
It's just stopping them
Doing the things
They want to do.
If you let them,
They let you.
People reply to threats
More actively
When not proposed as such.
For example,
I can let people take my hat
In a club,
Or break up a fight
When the opportunity is presented.
I don't mind if they do that,
As long as there's no pressure
To do things.
Leave us all some space
To be who we want to be.
Less conformity
More acceptance.
People on this planet
Vary wildly,
You have to accept that.
You have to accept that.
There will always be poor people.
People somewhere
Will always be oppressed.
But it changes.
Empires come and go

To and from this little rock.
We live through the rough
And through the smooth.
Where you are today
Is your luck.
Good or bad.
Take me for
Another example,
I am an addict
To the pursuit
Of complex relationships.
I like to be gratified.
By staring into eyes,
So clear,
You'd swear,
They couldn't lie to you.

How can I change my soul?
Do I even know what it is?
Is the fact
That I can follow,
Some predesigned plan
To ensure these exact thoughts
Are crossing your mind,
As you read this page?
Without hesitation
I accept my fate
And think in words
As they descend my forearms
Into my hands

Spreading to my fingers
Only to be scattered into the world
Via an interface
Rearranged linearly
On a screen in a font
All in a horizontal series.
Can life be so easy?
It seems that it is.
I am here and doing it,
Not whispering over your shoulder,
Despite the smoother interface,
You resist anyway,
Your morals have you by the balls.
Me, on the other hand,
I stand out enough
For people to believe me,
And as long as I can deliver the goods
They publicize more than any campaign.
People know about me
And the movement going on here,
And I become infamous
Before having sold
A single ounce of pain or ecstasy.

I need to reclude
To stop too many new events,
So I can catch up with the back log
Of things I take for granted
In my everyday life:
Jesus, with his free spirit

And dirty clothes,
The kind of man
Who approaches girls
When the music stops
Saying some shit like,
'Let's go fuck!'
Ariel with his antique house
And eclectic wardrobe,
His English cap
And unforgiving generosity.
The big muscly guy
And his whacked-out chicks.
The fat man,
His eight gangland murders
And his silver tooth,
His modern day piracy,
Dealing in groups in the clubs
Different man different task,
Slick too.
Slip with your Spanish
And receive a very firm,
'I don't know
What you are talking about.'
These things need to be
At least on the record,
If not in some publication,
A waiting list or production line.

It's getting on in the day,
Almost Friday faffle.

But we stick to the clock
And look for the three minutes
Before the change over
The warm up lap,
The finger exercises.
Get the blood everywhere
It is needed,
Get the neurones firing
Lead the way to some great creation
Of words and *frases*.

The intensity of an extended twinge
From a self plucked nose hair,
The flashing orange
The momentary monolateral blindness,
Dragged down by the solitary room
And the slow melancholy
The neo-blues musak.

This is the life
We are living.
Where Jesus is a hippie,
Wannabe drug dealer
Dancing with his arms to the heavens
And his pockets full of pills
Dancing like a seductive anti-cupid
In front of Max in the room today.
He is like smoke,
A phantom wisp
In the cobbled streets of San Telmo.

Then his evil twin brother,
Explodes in a cloud of dust
Into Caix and Pacha,
Paying the bills his smoky brother
Created in his real world reincarnation,
With kindness and *buena onda,*
Jesus is alive here in my little world.
He pushes pills and
Disrespects entire neighbourhoods
In single swooping statements.

Forget the speak of the six brothers,
Plus the one living in Andorra.
Exporting ecstasy home.
The others live the life,
Sliding thirty grams a week
Without battering an eyelid.
No problems either
Big strong lads
And several layers deep.
No flies on these guys
Think of the millions of miles
Further they would go
If they didn't have *pelo de concha*
Or *dos abuelos indiginos.*
Standing in front of shadowy doorways
Sunlight embossing their silhouettes,
Like some kind of superhero symbol.
His profile is stamped on the wall,
His personality soaks into the environment

He pulls its energy in
And balances the world out,
Riding what's available to him,
Always fitting in,
But never consciously,
Like a chameleon perhaps,
His emotions rise,
Triggering a chain reaction,
His skin tightens,
Drawing his cold blood inside,
Casting ash across his complexion.
And hiding his feelings from the world.
Josh recognises these people.
He calls them shape-shifters.
Fitting the expectations of the people
With whom they interact.
Nice guy gets treated well
Ladrón steals his hat
The wrath boils inside,
Whilst the exterior,
Hardens like ocean-poured lava.
Jesus can witness that.

Then there's Stjohn,
Of all the names, Stjohn
Call him San Juan
Just to simplify things
And keep vowels
Where they should be,
Between consonants,

Or in this case,
Between continents.
Another lost cause,
Just like Izu in Cairo
Born out of the world
Into the world
Without a world.
Neither border nor flag
Nation nor culture
To define
Just an accent and a passport,
Prejudice and paper.
If only he'd write.
I'd buy him a typewriter,
If I thought it'd get him going.
If he just pulled his finger out,
He would find something incredibly joyful,
The feeling of fingers
Combining with keyboard,
Interfacing,
Eating a naked lunch,
One that stands out.
This is why we live
To find the joy that affects us.
It's a probability thing.
Most things we read
Are either bad or irrelevant,
Driving us to explore,
In the hope of communicating
How differently the world can be,

Seen, described, experienced.
Those around us
Those who have lived
Find chains of fate
And by their fame,
Lose all neophilia.
Some are just stories
You've always had in your head.
You pick them up and read them,
When the time is right.
They push you
In the direction you need,
Or how else can you explain
The arrangement of 80,000 words
In such an order
That has such a profound effect
Moving a human being's life,
Their view of life,
And their desire to continue.

Get out, butterfly!
Lesbian seagull!
Bow down to the spliff-master,
Deep down and yes y'all.
Where does it come from?
Following the Friday
Keys and lighter
Saturday nighter.

I think this maybe the next one,

A really strong feeling.
The timing is just right,
The interruption,
The love affair,
The passionate withdrawal
Into romanticism,
The profundity unimaginable
From the outside world,
The entrance to ecstasy

I am starting a partnership
With this guy,
Dealing in legal tryptophans.
He ships them to me
And I peddle them to the pill heads
Here in the Good Air,
Then buy antiques
Watches and clothes,
Which we send back
Sell them in the States.
Wash our wallets,
Cut our profit,
Invest in product,
Then share the rest,
Share the love,
On a Sunday morning,
By the river,
Exploring new sensations
Of ecstasy.

I kind of feel that
By telling you this,
I am also telling you
We're drifting apart.
We've both met other people
To fill the huge wholes
We've left in each others' sides,
And I am glad of that
For both our sakes.
We can be happy apart.
I miss you,
But knowing you're entertained
By someone who reminds you of me
Is heart warming enough.

I am into this other girl now.
She will fall in love.
The shy, quite-quiet type.
She'll flourish under my wing,
I'll teeter on the event horizon,
Of her black-hole pupils
Parked in balance
Soaking up the love they emit,
The crystality of their gaze,
Their intoxifying rays.
Until repetition befalls us,
Then I'll invent a fantasy story,
Her little sister perhaps.
You know who I'm talking about,
You've all come across one

And you know about mine.
I'll seize any opportunity
Any chance to go to your home,
Search for the girl,
Having chosen a day
When we'll be alone,
Just me and her in the house
I'll have come to collect some things,
Stuff I left in the boxes
In the other room.
No, I won't be long
But I can stop by for a while
And drink a *mate* or something,
Sitting in the kitchen perhaps,
Or on that futon,
For irony's pitiful sake,
On that futon.
Talking,
Smiling,
Intoxicating,
Introducing her to my wicked side,
And the stories I have to tell
About my new friends
Who populate my world
With the colour of their lies.
She'll be bewitched
By the places I talk of
And the emphasis I place,
By their ability
To fill people with energy,

To excite those same pleasure centres,
To which we are slaves.
And then she'll give into me,
Give me my moment of *ecstasis,*
The pure pleasure of being told
What love means
In the words of someone close.
Then wanting to admit
Something sordid to them.
To the first person you meet after,
How I feel that way about,
The flash of lost innocence
The bitter acceptance of those parts of life,
That aren't easily explained.
Then relax into a state of placidity and love,
Fulfil the desire to be held and touched,
Caressed and stroked,
Collapsing into each others' arms
And consuming the naked flesh.

I am,
As you often tell me,
A consumer.
If not *the* consumer.
I produce nothing but empty words,
Whore to the page,
Yet spend, spend, spend
Daily, weekly, nightly
Fort-nightly.
Until crisis befalls me.

This week is a case in point.
I haven't even expended energy
In pursuit of consumption.
Five days in the bed,
A four-hour outing on Monday
Was enough to make me ill.
Between times to be in heaven
And times to be in the lake,
I now wallow in shallow waters,
Breed creativity and strength,
Rebuild my weakened self
For the things to come.
First things first,
I plan to fall in love soon,
Another strain on the body
So I'll need to be strong,
To prepare and to eat well,
Take care of my serotonin levels,
Hanging out with all these crazy chicks.
Gonna to be real famous soon too,
Gonna have to be looking good,
Better take some spas and sunbeds,
Make sure we don't come out all pasty,
Wouldn't wanna be all washed up
When the paparazzi arrive.
Gonna be a hectic few weeks,
Gonna be spending a lot of time
Doing a lot of mashed up talking.
That's tough on the mouth.
It's delicate tissue inside there.

Only other place you find skin like that,
All soft and gentle
Is on the genitalia.
Take my word on that one,
Not something you can just overlook.
Then there's the drugs,
We'll be doing a lot by nasal means.
Gonna damage the membranes,
Exposing us to high probabilities of infection,
Gonna get crazy up in here
But we're
Gonna have the edge,
Walking around,
Talking about how,
I just dropped the Sause.
It's the new drug
Josh has been all crazy about.

I know he has a stash,
Hidden somewhere,
It might even be in his case.
I'll go check.
Nothing
About to write
Two a.m. and still waiting,
But I think
I'm already feeling something.
And it is two a.m.
The connection
With the keyboard

Is there.
I can feel it.
I was also about to write
A note about how it felt.
So right in the moment
So whatever I tell you
I took it in the right mood.
Everything was perfect.
I felt a little guilty.
About not taking it with Ariel.
But I think that even
If he was that upset,
We could convince Adrien
To loan us his,
Until we get some more.

Anyway I took it
With good intentions.
I was even thinking
About writing something cool.
If this drug is
As new as you say it is,
Then it's bound
To abound
In creative potential
For the arts, I mean.
I am convinced,
I've seen Josh's paintings
His doodles
Those things!

He says they're just to stop him
From going all crazy,
Stop him from losing his shit,
Stop him from becoming
Another brain zombie.
That guy is free.
He's the most free fucker out there,
Besides Jesus,
That is.
He just dropped his dirty pants
On the States,
Sat butt-naked
On a plane seat
Dumped out his last bowl of oatmeal,
Then started living it up here
He didn't even bring his cool clothes,
He just tapped into a new fashion
Five minutes off the plane.
Now people are stealing his shit
Just to look like him.

Two o'five
It's getting a little crazy
On the keyboard side of things,
A little slanty.
The typing is going off
A little.
There is no music,
I should sort that out

While I still can.

Two o'nine
Now I feel twisted out of my shit,
Returning to this slanty keyboard
Is like something comfortable
And familiar,
For a minute.
Now it's the same scary shit,
The inapproachability,
The amount of faith
I have to expend
To get out the words I want.

It's a balance
Between my attention
To the keys,
And the fluidity of my brain,
Which seems to be
Failing me now.
I slow down
Really feeling my sides
Fill up like balloons inflated.
But I am feeling ill still,
I am coughing,
Half expecting
To vomit something black
Like I've heard about this stuff.
You're beautiful,
And I'm twisted off my shit,

Completely gone,
The words are like a movie screen.
I feel like they are printed
On a huge screen
In front of a crowd
Of a million little fingers
And keyboard keys.
A little Fred Astaire dances
Across the screen train,
Led by my words
In back and white,
Flat-screen trinitron vision

I said I'd do something
Really nice for Josh,
After I made him my slave
For a week.
So I am going to,
I'm going to dedicate
Whatever I get from this
Experience to him,
Not just in an acknowledgement
In the beginning
Or the hint of his name,
But openly and sincerely
Dedicate this as a piece of art
As a present to him.
Not because it may have any value
But because I like to give,
And I know he is going

To enjoy the fuck
Out of having supplied
The drug that has created
This nonsense.

Or can we turn it around,
Hack together some sham
Of a novella,
That's a twenty minute novel,
Or get my hands
On nineteen more hits,
Write a chapter a day.
Has to make some money.

Has to be fun researching.
It's a one off,
Buy the drugs,
Take them continuously
Until the book is finished.
It's a marvel of the drug,
Your interaction
With nothing
In the universe
Except the keyboard.
Everything in slow motion,
Every keystroke becoming perfect,
As if some silk-clad ballet
Of coordination slid things
Over the page
With a slicken glossiness

Of everything and the world
Just flowing
Through my finger tips.

Reality is re-emerging slightly,
Really being pulled back
Into a world for minute.
I crave objectivity.
That was a rush
That may come back,
Or it maybe a sign
Of things to come.
Thirty minutes in
At tops,
Perhaps less,
Overarching characteristic
Is intimacy with the keyboard.
Perhaps *hasta hablar*
En otra idioma
También puede ser
Si las palabras
Salen facilimente
Tan facil como las inglesas?
Pero en chiste
Digo.
This is a place
Of immense pleasure.
I wish
I could
Invite all my friends.

It's warm and fuzzy
A little buzzy
And twingly in the tuzzy

A little later in,
It's getting more crazy.
I'm having to hold desires back.
I'm doing it
But I am feeling things inside,
Thumping and energy,
Maybe to dance.
It seems very delicate,
Because I am ill still.
Perhaps later in the experiment,
We will find out
If it is more dancey.
If it supplies energy
In such a direct way.
It seems to energise
My weak frame.
I need more days
Of rest
Before I can begin
To think about my plans
For falling in love
At the weekend.
I need to take care of myself
Be prepared.

Completely gone.

Two-twenty-five,
Managed to drink *jarabe*
To calm my cough.
Direct effect
With no direct side effect
Images now flood forth.
The *alucinógeno*
The trippin-ass part
It's strange to think
That this soft fabric
With which I interact
Is all part of the same thing.
So sexy
Typing words on my lap
Getting excited,
By the luxury,
Of the sensuality,
Of the moment.

It turned very sexy
For a minute.
I feel out of touch,
Because I keep coming back
To write about it.
I really don't want to fall
Into one of these fantasies,
Then lose myself.
I want to explore
Diversity of paths,
Then let other people

Investigate each direction.
This moment in time
Has been predestined.
We've all seen it.
Many things have led to it,
And it has the same *lindoness*
That the world has right now.
So it all just slots into place
Almost like a good speed-x diet,
But you have to balance shit right
Just outside the perfect mix
Lie two grey areas
Of bad parties,
Outside there's coke
And m.d.m.a.
A spliff or two,
When shit's bad,
Some keta too.
But most attempts
Are just scrabbling wishes,
Regret mounting
On some velvet morning.

The keyboard falls away.
Like an a.t.m.
I can't control it.
It's slightly precarious.
The letters imprint,
Then fall away.
I just stay in connection

With them all the time
To make this recording
As fruitful as possible.
We should all be learning
From these types of drug
And experience.
All of the positive
Nice lovely
Novelty things
A trip through life
Can bring us.

It seems like
I am thinking more
Than I really am.
Am I going
Through severe memory loss
Or is my time consciousness
Failing me hard.
Is this freshly created space
Filling with rubbish.
Things that really
Have never happened
To me
Are slotting in,
Fleshing out my mind,
Replacing a meticulous archive
With a file system
Of memory.
Loosely hooked together.

As if by magic,
I have a new history
Like I just woke up
In a new world
In a town
Of new people
New faces and places.
I am transformed to
Whichever person on the planet
To see the world
From their eyes in that moment.
Loco!
Muy loco!

Look do I really care

I'll throw in statements
Into the middle of nowhere
To prove an argument to you.
Excuse me
I am having an inane argument
With my self over nothing.
I hope you are enjoying this
As much as I am.
If so, let me tell you a story,
About the world's most famous screenwriter.
So famous
They made a movie of his fingers
Typing words on the screen.
Now lie watching

The première of that movie,
Shown in his honour
Wherever he wants it
To be shown
With whoever he wants to be with.

I tell the girls it's me
And that I'm with them,
Because they're the new girl
Of my dreams.
Not my one,
The one I've been craving,
Talking about all week
As my girl,
The way I do.
I always hype things,
Especially girls
I always hype girls
So they are famous
When they come into my social group,
So they are welcomed in
Treated like they should be.
Gently warmed nest.
Such loveliness
Like the entire duration
And complication of a life
Was all here just for the sake
Of theses hours
Of drugged hallucinations
Are going to produce what worth

Awards? Medals?
Money? No.
Even recognition
Is a stretch.
But who cares?
All objectors are objected to.
They're force fed an exception
And must accept our agenda,
To have fun,
To party hard,
Or just at all.
For that matter,
Or just be pleasureful
Whatever choice is ours
And we are going to take it.
Let us be,
We are like it now,
There is little that I fight against
But perhaps others
Could be freed up a little.
What do I know
This is just like the movies.
It doesn't seem like life.
I can just a dance
Across town
Across the keyboard,
A finger exercise
A workout
For the creative centres
Of my brain,

A drug that clears out
Black boxes
Makes people repetitive
Without their knowledge,
Or consent,
A long-term side-effect,
Even now it's trying
To trick me out of writing these words.
I fight the hallucinations.
It doesn't want the truth
To be revealed.
But I believe
The drug is making
Us repetitive.
It could be a conspiracy
Invented by the spies…
Of course.
Then push it in the streets,
It'd be a huge addiction,
And would leave a happy electorate
To enjoy their hormone fed steak sandwich.

Two forty-seven, *muy loco*.
Sounds are tripping out now too.
Well into the heavy shit now.
Still riding it,
But cool as a *gata*.
No need to peak or dive,
But I have that peak power
In my side cupboard

To over control that shit.
We can dive and fly,
Loop the fucking loop
With this shit,
And some weed and coke
Maybe even a little coke spliff
Probably a little dangerous
Up in here,
But it's a historical reference.
Its usage was popular at this time.
You can quote this,
Feeling choked up.
This maybe a personal thing
As I have eaten lots this week,
Filled out my exhausted g.i. tract
For the first time in a long one.
So I feel like I should explode
But warm and comfortable
Peaceful
Like this was the right time.

Bear in mind
Twenty or say days of this
Is probably a price
I can't pay.
I call it a price
But it's fun really,
Talking about fatigue,
And metabolistic destruction.
If I have to keep jumping

Out of the high
To put food in my gut,
Words down on the page,
I guess then it is a price.
Not really riding waves
Or am I?
The fantasy wave
That is my life,
The one I've always
Wanted to live.
Is that just fantasy
Or can this really be
Considered a job
Do I enjoy this?
Process putting words paper?
Come on!
You know me!
You should answer this!
This is who I am.
Take me
As you fucking-well find me.
I run this town
Upside down,
And I wont turn around
If you don't look back down,
Like I fall for a girl
Every week.
But I ain't fallen
For a girl like this one
In a long time,

Two long years
I would try and stop me from saying.

Two fifty-seven
For the record
I'm twisted off my shiiiiiiiiiiiiiiiiiiit
And did this consciously,
For recreational and creative purposes.
I am having fun
Up inside this body unit.

I am lost now.
It's all the same fabric.
Just the intensity has augmented,
The world and the keyboard
Are the same fabric,
Warm, soft and easy to manage.
I can type slowly onto the page.
The words slide sexually
And smoothly from the slithery
Slips of skin and the ends of
The fingers of my hand
As they say.

Let's blow this one wide.
We'll call it the Sause Diaries.
There will be no sly back hand talk.
It will be straight up,
About a new drug
That is called Sause.

And it's good and legal
And you should try it.
While it remains that way
Use it properly
And we can all get along
Like fluffy turds in a basket,
And be lead
On a little walk
Through the velvety and oak
Clad chambers of the mind,
Always well-furnished.
An apartment in Russell Square,
Late 19th century
Or stretching contemporary,
The Rio Metro
And its seventies' orange retro.
A bit of revival
For our survival.
But textured and refined,
Well read and reserved,
For a gentle bred well man
Whose inside of the mind
Is fitted like a Rolls Royce.
A journey of words
Through the mind
In the luxury comfort,
Is a pleasurable journey
For us all.
I hope you are seated comfortably,
The brain is ready for departure,

Travelling faster than I can keep up.
Will I have to slow things down
To absorb everything?
Is this slow or too fast?
I can't tell if it's sped up,
Or the world slowed down.
I can't keep up
I have to pause.
I hope you are happy mutherfucker.
You put me into a really fucking cool place.
I am twisted from my spixle.
I wish you was here to see it.
This is the best I can leave for you.
This you can bring
Your squizzled brain back to.

The keyboard is what I really
Feel in touch with.
It's warm and has the same
As everything else
The t.a.m. t-i-n,
For example,
With the coke
It's cold and horrible,
Making my words go all over,
Because I don't want to touch it
Where it is
In front of the keyboard.
This is how happy you made me,
That I am writing it to you

In your own fucking language,
Here I am actually thinking it out
Like you don't know it
Reading a manual
To something that you push on me.
Just wait until I do this coke
Gonna be off the hooooook.

I am going to lose my shit.
Am I really ready for this?
Just a lick of the card got me wiffled.
Care now,
I don't want to fry the circuits
Beyond linguistic capability.

I want to record this
To make it something,
A journey,
A meditation,
A message into the mind
Of a lost soul.
Why am I here?
Why we are here?
Living it up,
With Jesus and Ariel,
In our little custom-made paradise.
The world we would have created
For ourselves.
A world where we are fed
By nothing by pure luxury,

Living in the most dire of squalor,
Where even being ill
With a dying cough
Ends up being in a movie
By the end of the week,
Twisted out of your shit on Sause

As if someone created it
Just for us.
Little pieces of white
Rolled up paper
With apartments or rooms for rent
On the back
Holding me back
From greatness.
I could type at one word per day
And still write
The Rolls Royce of novels
On this shiny old keyboard.
It's like a well warn
But still warm carpet
But I can't find
That stupid wrap of paper
When I need nasal stimulant
For a bigger drug rush
Here in my craziness.
You were right,
It is fun.
This is the proof,
A verbal snapshot

From inside the mind of a Sause head.

Ok!
Stop!
I have got to the point
Where I am looking for a roll,
But thinking
Oh but I could drop the Sause
That would be a great right now.
That's *déjà vu* right?
There is a certain truth
Hanging in the matrix right now,
Bashing my head
Every time we roll past it.

Perhaps it's just a normal drug trip.
It has the funny parts,
Serotonin levels etcetera.
But then other times,
You just say, why bother,
I'm tired and struggling
Like the rest of us.
But then I don't feel it
The day later,
Like a transient in and out
Of other peoples lives.
Really I am lost inside
Of an entire world by this place.
The world seems like
A Chinese hanging work of art.

The type of life you see
Through the mountains and mist
Through the trees and cloud.
Fuzzy and taken care of by good Dao

Three twenty, reminded of the time
By the music,
Something special in this song
Makes me remember
That the c.d.
Will soon end,
Or rewind to the beginning
And go through the same songs over and over,
Giving me hint of repet….
In my trip that is,
Not in the words,
Little pieces of unrolled up
Paper keeping me
Back from greatness,
I'm in this world
Above the others,
The movie world
Where I'm glossy and brilliant,
Big and strong,
Good looking,
In charge.
Everything turns out smoothly,
As if James Bond himself
Had meticulously planned it.
I am the martial art westerner,

The super cool cat
In a bohemian lifestyle,
Ready to break out
Some juicy dance floor moves,
Push a little x
To my lovely friends,
And have a doog time partying
Down here in Buenos Aires,
The Good Air.
With all the southern folk,
Talking about craw-fish and pussy.

It is a bit jittery right now.
The spliff makes all smoother.
I am in between the drugs.
There's just a little of the coke left.
I can put it in a joint
To blend smoothly across,
Or see how I go on the withdrawal.
Off coke,
Then some coke,
Then some weed,
Then more weed.
Will it last long enough
To do all those who should
Try the smooth blend,
Dive in head first.
Try out this new sports shoe!
It's called sause.
Take a few laps around the track

Explore the texture
Write a few notes.

Josh must have written lots
Of this shit in this state.
We should dig some of it out,
Clean it up,
Unearth some real gems of human behaviour.
I just love hearing his stories
About getting girls
To eat each other out
On Bourbon Street.
O' New Orleans!
I just want to see it.
I'd go for two fat chicks.
Out of my mind.
Well the rolled up paper
Is no longer holding me back
And I am still going,
Enjoying this to the maximum.
Whatever purpose it will serve
Is slowly becoming harder to perceive.
It is slowly becoming less useful,
Perhaps in the end it will just serve
To be laughed at.

Three thirty the music did stop,
And it has made a difference.
The music is definitely connected to the drug
It's not that essential things

Are clearer without it,
For example.
But you want to clear your head up
You just turn off the music.
It all clears up.
You get out what you
Need to get out.
And then,
If you're feeling in the mood,
Put the music back on.
It's totally relaxed like that.
You're allowed to do
Whatever you want.
But they still have them
All brainwashed with the drug,
There's a purpose
To the entire hallucination.
In that you have to write
A really convoluted plot
About a conspiracy drug
That makes you repeat yourself
Over and over.
Chronically your real life,
Inescapably you go crazy.
And draw little scribbly imblius lines
And spell things badly
On purpose
Until you can no longer think.
Then they will just
Feed off your brain juice

To keep their super inventions cold
Thanks to this cerebral fluid.
Muy loco.
That hasn't stopped.
I am still thinking in terms of the day.
There is a definite justice to the words
I have inside,
A real connection to the drug
And to my friends.
None of them are here,
But I can supply to them whatever they need.
I am plugged into their world.
Where I'm most comfortable,
I can control everything.
And I will always feel
Like I love all the people
I want to love equally.
Only when I am truly happy,
Whether that is here or not
Is unimportant.
Like worship
Is necessary for a church.
But it's *muy loco*
Have to put on some music.
I have to.
Now I think about relaxing my jaw,
Perhaps the marijuana will calm things out.
I can handle trippy,
Just not fast or dancey.
I might go

With some slow trancey
Chilled out stuff,
Maybe Coldplay,
Relax to some good *onda,*
Enjoy some of these visuals,
Explore the mind's creative side,
Find how wide opened up
This drug has made it.
There's a lot off fuzzy warm energy
Pouring in.
I refine it to powerful poetry,
Feelings of grandeur,
Focus.
Off the scale of things
Going on inside my brain
It's all very circular.
Just a drug
Leaving people drawing circles
In pens with their lives
Everywhere in life
Just drawing circles
And the odd dot or line.
Like a Hollywood ice movie
It just keeps getting longer and longer
It's an epic before you know it.
Just for my friend Josh
To while away his Virginia hours
While he reads his twisted kids
Brain vomit of the Sause.
That's rearranged his perceptions

Of the interfacableness of reality.
For so long been submerged
In thinking he was a hot dog.
Perhaps now he will follow the path.
Followers will follow him
In not following well-trodden paths.
In so doing, find and follow
Our own individual path and
Muy loco debe estar,
Muy loco esa droga,
Mirame la cara,
Hecha mierda.
Really gone and stupid.
Need music and reality.
Sause twisted my shit.
I'm so happy,
And I'm writing again.

The fabric changes
All the time.
But I don't leave the connection
Just get a lot of noise.
To be tidied up later.
As long as the main signal
Is getting through
The finger tips
The instructions
All correctly interpreted
Once you have this,
You will write

And everything will be ok.
Like a message typed
By god's long legged
blond, knickerless assistant,
Sat cross legged on the king size
At home.
What a secretary,
She penned it herself
Whilst taking a moment's breather
From am elegant fantasy massage
Of her clitoris.
I don't like the repetitiveness of this Sause
It will be my first complaint
I seem to go in circles
Perhaps I need some entertainment
I know you will come back soon
That will be fun.
I will sop writing then.
I know this too.
That's why I write,
Over and over now
To squeeze it out
I know it's a long job.
Twenty days of this
Maybe less repetitive
I know I have to do it
I do it all this week.
Now the words flow
So easily it will get easier
It's not speed reading or speed writing.

It's just being in flow
With life.
Having the same connection,
Being really drugged up.
Just recording every thought
As it passes though my brain
As if I were some in a matrix of thought
And the screen is just another place
Of pre-presentation of my *pensamientos*.
It's just that I want them to be here
For all people to read
That's why I have attached myself
Metaphysically and physically
With a machine of common language
Where I can leave the stupidity
Of this drug all over it
So people can bear witness
To its complete insanity
The kind of shit it does to a brain.
Why would anybody not love
How fucked this gets you?
I need a t-shirt man.
Reading, 'Sause whacked
My shit
Out of all proportion.'
I'm in incredible euphoria,
A sensation that
Every point of my entire life
Has been leading up to this moment,
This point of being

These interconnections,
Between so many disjointed thoughts
The unity of my being
My wholeness.
This is a good place to be
Anywhere.
If you can feel like this,
Wherever you look around,
You're comfortable with people
Who will support you,
Look after you,
Give you Sause,
When you're feeling ill
And have planned it
A million thought circles prior.
A true testament
To my ability
To test the circuits
Of my testability.

This shit is *muy loco*
Muy circular
Everything in my life
Has been leading to this point
Like the basis of my movie,
Everything is really good.
My friends come.
It will be lovely,
Like the ecstasy poem.
And all the other million events,

Of my life.
That will probably end up,
Jumping onto this page.
I have keyboard diarrhoea.
I have the coke spliff ready.
Everything is seeming
Like it was meant to be.
The drug or reality.
Josh was having considerations
About staying another weekend
In bad-ass Buenos Aires.
I don't hesitate
This weekend I am gonna fall back in love,
I've been out too long.

Intense intense pleasure,
Thinking about serotonin maintenance
Cos' were hanging out
With some crazy chicks
The soundtrack to my life.
The verbal recreation,
Or reproduction
Of the convoluted and twisted.

Sause off brain main mind
Be careful!
You boy,
You're coming out
To write things.

Of the real world,
Not dragging the world,
Into this little fantasy drug trip of yours.
It's a verbal slurrrr diary,
Not a piece of art.
Twenty more are due,
Twenty days of repeatability,
Then no more drug.
We're manufactured minds now,
Thinking that everything is circular,
Making us cocaine consumers,
Using our money
To fund their investigation
Into small robotic futuristic type shit.
That's fine by me,
They can do that,
If they want
Just so long as it doesn't affect
The damn price of oranges.
They can do what they want,
That's ok.
As long as there's coffee and juice,
Delivered by sirens of Buenos Aires
Every morning.
Whatever we have to do
To keep the level of service up.
Where's my cocaine?
On plastic cleavage mutherfuckers.
You need to spread the love.
I need to build the lines.

Here I am twisted off my shit,
Needing to take shit
Gonna be fun.
Thinking in circles *es muy loco.*
You might be going back into fast,
This might be too fluxy
For people,
Might not catch the grip
Of what you're saying.
You see how the words
Are just not slick enough
To follow the reality,
The hollywoodness of Buenos Aires
Right now
Is beyond all appreciable levels.
We are just in the glitz capital of the world.
We do whatever the fuck we want,
Wherever we are,
Whenever we want.
Like it's just crazy,
We have no limits,
The money seems to flow and flow,
The parties get better,
We look prettier,
We get more girls,
We have more fun,
Finding out deeper things
About the universe,
And all that,
Without having even

Smoked the spliff yet,
Or thought about the next four hours,
The next ten,
Or whatever time you get back
Bound to be late and coked up
And ready to unleash.
I am going to be a time bomb of talking.
You can be the Nagasaki of ears.
You can feel the words bursting out of me,
This is a new literary sensation.
Feel these words,
Bite your tight flesh,
Let them tease you
Tickle you to that mood.
That you like,
Feel the innocence.
Of reading words and feeling good.
The pleasure of being literate,
Self-sufficient on the page.
Slide back into the foamy reassurance
That life will support us
On whatever ventures we take
Or even fall into,
That whatever happens
We are supported
From underneath by the fabric
The pleasure of being ill
Sick of everything.

Four o'eight twisted still off

The Sause, my shit.
Trying to record everything
From a trip
As a first testament,
My last recalling moment of sanity.
Since then everything became involved,
My entire life,
Part of this hallucinogenic web,
A new sensation of pleasure.
You won't understand this,
It's too fast and too circular,
A different experience and Sause.

Four fifteen grandeur is the path
Sanity the vehicle.
A low noise to signal ratio.
The Sause's challenge.
We can get a good record,
Two hours.
The fabric is still here.
I am still watching
The movie in my head,
Now smoking a spliff
Watching it,
Experiencing more noise.
Smoke then type.
Everybody talks about Sause.
It's the reason we're all here,
To take it and be in the same fabric.
We accept people of the fabric,

Although it's hard to smuggle in
Writing instruments.
I'm working undercover.
They're all out having fun.
I sneaked this laptop in
Under the covers of this velvet world.
These words are contraband
From the country of desire.
The palace of pleasure
Residing in Sause heaven
Looking at what Sause brings you.
Everybody wants Sause.
It's the shit.
It's the most self-satisfying
Complacency riddled,
Mind-repeating
Drug ever.
It is probably set
To take over the world.
And we are the only people
Lucky enough to get it pure,
Unprogrammed
And in the city of pure pleasure.
The pleasure of being ill.
What privilege
We're really grateful.
Living out days
Of pure pleasure
In this bitch.
He will testify to that

Good ol' god.
They haven't noticed yet
But I must be careful.
If they come in,
Find me recording my Sause experience
They will surely throw me out.
My last days in Argentina
They won't let me re-enter
Something here is significant.
Can I play the paranoia trip on Josh?
Can I trust he isn't c.i.a.?

Four twenty four, aware of paranoia.
Extent obvious in writing.
Everything else under control,
Just resurfacing
To write the following report:
This is enlightenment.
The point in time
Where everything is just everything
For the sake of being.
Everything held in suspension.
The support of definition.
Everything has its purpose
To serve its purpose.
Nothing is unbalanced.
Everything just is
Frozen in a moment in time
On the sause
Twisted off my shit.

Yeah, euphoria!

Should I really be freely smuggling
This drug out of its world?
Or should I just be saving it
For special people.
Not giving
Everyone.
They shouldn't all have to.
It's all seeing

Not everything was meant to be
In this moment.
I can almost feel
Sun and sin
Coming down over me.
I feel everything
Just supposed to be,
Except the writing shouldn't be here.
It's the one thing
Standing in the way.
I feel like I have smuggled
This out of its world.
Shouldn't the recording instrument
Be pulled into the society,
Interfaced directly,
Used to record discourse
Dialogue.
Moments of pure behaviour.
Yet here everything is reversed,

Saused sause diaries.
Are societies being dragged
Into the recording instrument
Through the medium of brain juice?

Four thirty-six, on top of the world,
Twisted off my shit on Sause.

Four thirty-nine spliff is finished,
Still in control
Just writing a circular report.
This could be called Circusause.
You know people will think
It is the kind of source Sause.
Or even spelt Sauce.
Really plainly
With no imagination.
Is the signal getting through?
Without too much fabric noise
Don't forget I am very ill
While making this recording.
The Sause
For Joshua, you old pal, you
Choripan provider.

I am in complete control
Of every moment on Sause.
I control all this in a flash.

Only four forty,

But I have travelled
Through a trillion galaxies,
In those hundreds of seconds,
Onto another level
Where everything is just enlightened,
Where the only word is 'enlightened,'
The true word of being,
In complete control of the universe.
It's got to be special
To be here so soon
After having been thrust
Into the world of the living
For so long.
Or so short,
It's impossible to tell.

This might sound rather strange
To the person reading
Not having crossed the matrix barrier.
Take the pill
When offered to you.
You'll never look back,
No point in returning
Past the point of no return
To being the same again!
Here's a different world.
Here you are free and balanced.
People will carry you on pills
Jesus having a good *onda*.
This is the heaven of the earth.

This is paradise.
The sause is the music.
Thumping *Buenos* into a bad ass city
Thanks to all my friends,
All the gang.
From here we edit life.
We are so in control
Lives so forecastable.
Due to desire,
Just playing the game.
I want to do this.
I go and do it.
Just completely in control
Of everything.
Totally on another level
In a place where we can just hang out,
Do a bunch of coke
Talk about going south,
Talk about craw-fish and pussy,
But never having to set on a porch,
Smoking a whole bunch of weed,
And relaxing.
We just say it.
Then we go do it.
Make a rapid oral list.
Say it and do it.
Like dealing out the cards
From inside the casino.
The feeling of being on the winning side.
The side calling the shots.

I want good music,
Fun drugs and crazy chicks.
I want to hang out with crazy artists,
Draw a bunch of pictures
And give them to my new friends,
Give them hippie names and explanations
Say something like 'I just do it,
To get the demons out
That's all.'
Talking with guys like Jesus and Ariel
Not even speaking the same language
But communicating simple things.
I can tell he is as cool as fuck
He knows I am cool
And that I have the sause.
And people like him are allowed
Into the Sause club,
When they access the sause
Or the pleasurable things we desire,
We touch down into the world
With the interactions of our auras
While away time.
Talking shit
About stuff,
I just say that and I go do it,
No problem,
Without even thinking about it.
I be in there,
Enjoying life,
Being in control.

I mean when you can get it
As easy as swallowing this one Sause pill,
Crossing over into the land
Of an unknown pleasure,
You will be loving me
For recommending it to you
Whilst it remains legal.
After that, it'll be something else.
Point is,
You need to explore yourself.
This is how I manifest.
This recommendation to you
In the form of this transcript
From inside the Sause.
I send it to you
In some circular twisted
Off the matrix shit
In order to be able
To help bring more people
Into touch with themselves
Into touch with the Sause.
I think they're trying to cut me off.
I will go do some everyday things
Like take a pee and wash maybe,
Have a shower,
Throw them off the scent,
Pass some time being normal,
Relaxing and shaking off their trail,
Cool down the laptop,
Spend a bit of time re-interacting

With the Sause fabric.
Maybe I started writing too quickly.

Four forty-six, have lost control
Of who is exactly in control of what
In the Sause.
Fucked off my bad ass shit with Sause
Gonna love this, good god.

Four forty-nine, thinking maybe
They have all taken Sause.
And I am now the last to join the club,
Or the new member,
Still bringing cool people,
Who have things to share,
With the partiers here in Buenos Aires.
The Good Air is free here.
We provide
What the people need.
They provide us with what we need.
In other words the weed,
We just have to bring the Sause,
You and me buddy.
We take over the world,
Control the entire shit.
Sell the Sause,
Eat coke off bad-ass bitches' titties,
Gobble some steaks and have fun,
Hangout with out friends,
Order fresh chori's

From the front of the grill,
Do a bunch of fun stuff,
Draw some whacky pictures,
Give them to our friends,
Write about them in circular circles
Of pure Sause.
On the Sause everything is different.
Everything is like
It's been preparing for me
And me for everything,
The easy life,
Complete luxury and pure pleasure.
Have to take a piss
I go.
Everything is just so pleasurable here,
So much like paradise,
Nothing is far away,
Everything you have ever learned
Is close by.
The places you love
Are easy to visit.
There are serene images of placidity,
Every memory connected to pleasure.
And pleasure connected to every memory,
Every single part of my life
Has served a purpose
In my being here
Doing this
Right now.
I've lived my entire life

For this moment,
Have even been writing a novel
With the theme based on a person,
Writing his entire life story
In the space of one evening.
It seems a little improbable
That it's all improbable,
After all the improbable talk
Of noise and static and things
Blocking this sause reading.

Five o'two, forced to clean
The top of the coke tray
For gum fodder.
Coked up I realized
The tin, the card and the Sause
And everything else
For that matter
Was all there for a purpose.
I enjoyed the hell out of that thought.
It's off the hook.
I just had sex with time.
I was licking that trim box
Talking about pussy taking Buenos Aires,
Let me talk shit to my friends,
Let me do my art o' the Sause.
Don't control me,
Let me do all this the stuff .
I want to let me do it, Sause.
Let me write and hang out

With these guys
In the South
In the Good Air.
I want to hang out there,
Talk to a lot a crazy people,
Worry about my serotonin levels,
Be a hippy,
Take a bunch of Sause,
Or just swap it for a bunch of pills,
And then go do those instead.
Cocaine maybe makes me bad,
Makes me enjoy the evil pleasures
Of the world,
And now of the Sause,
Remember Joshua
It's Sause with an 's.'
It's kind of fabricky in here.
I am not sure.
He laughs how can he not be sure.
This is the most fabricky it's ever gotten.
Living in San Telmo,
Doing what we want,
In the back drop
From a Lara Croft Venice scene.
Do as you please
Enjoy your stay,
Argentinian style hotel.
Just hanging out and having fun,
Introducing people like Max
To the sause and having fun,

Controlling all sorts of movements,
Being artistic and unique,
Generally giving art away
To our friends,
Because we like the Sause
and having fun on it.

Five twelve, on this sause recording
Everything is lovely and alright.
The sun is shining in the form of a bulb
But it's the same light as Caix.
It's the same light as Ibiza
It's the light of ecstasy.
It radiates in the hearts of some of us,
And we are here to liberate
The rest from the matrix
With the Sause pill.
We are going to give them this high,
This repetitive suspension
Of all problems,
Save the noise to signal ratio,
Which will be cleared up
By our team of mad monkey scientists
To reveal this recording of madness.
It's the Sause.
This is a document of fabric,
Of just doing things,
So as to avoid going crazy.
Because we are so in control
Of our entire lives right now.

We have freed ourselves using the Sause.
It's probably why they said do it
At a good time,
Or you might get stuck forever.
I know it was pleasurable before.

Five fourteen, the trip is a little worrying.
The sublimity of the ecstasy is unforgiving.
It leaves a solitude
Marked by the how
Of will I pass the rest
Of eternity
In this moment
At this speed.
The exasperation of everything
The limitlessness of having everything,
Absolutely every single last part
Of your human experience,
So close to hand.
Once you are here,
Everything that makes you feel good
Is also there.
You need nothing.
It's euphoria,
Pure and simple,
In the sause
.twisted.
Off my shit
Ok

Five seventeen, coming back into control
Less twisted and more sensed.
I have realised that I have escaped
Hopefully with my recording,
And definitely with an enhanced sense
Of awareness
Of my powers,
What I can and can't do,
In this real world,
The pleasures I can expect,
The dues I have to pay
In return,
So I can balance the entirety
And smoke a spliff
Twisted off my shit on the Sause.

Five twenty, speaking of time,
You have a warm watch
In your crotch,
Like it was ordered
By double-o seven himself.
The coincidences keep colliding,
Undivided un-re-guiding,
Lovingly balanced.
This recording is not to promote Sause,
Despite it all fitting so well into place,
The Maxiness of it all
Completely stops confounding
The Sause taker.
I feel like I knew

That everything was always
Going to be ok,
And now it just is,
And it's no big deal,
So we just hang out,
Take Sause.
It's legal.
We can always just order a bunch,
Maybe I will need to take it again,
Perhaps it won't always be the same,
In such lovely form,
Such perfect control.
How does that work?
Do I go up from here,
Or down from there?
Muy loco
Digo yo.
¡Eh!
Muy loco
Es very *especial,*
Just for you.
I know that
Just by taking this drug,
I can make some people happy.
They'll know that we've all done it,
Have the same knowledge
Of these bigger things.
They'll realise what's going on
And join us taking Sause,
Talking shit.

I guess you don't need
To keep taking it.
It's the initial enlightening
That's needed.
Anything else
Might slow us down
In our adult selves.
The point of growth,
The extension of being,
The entire point of happiness,
Droning on for hours,
Talking shit,
About things you don't even
Want to hear about,
Until you come across the Sause,
Decide upon it,
The fabric,
The extension of love,
Fuelled by the trytophanic effect
On serotonin in the brains,
While taking Sause.
It's a long-ass life induction,
But severely worthwhile
Since you get in return
Enlightenment.
It all seems right
Together when you are inside,
Entirely free of everything
Paused in control of the Earth.
I still have to deal

With other people,
But not until later.
I can feel it coming.
I will control my shit.
Ariel had it easy when he was..
Had it easy *qué* easy?
Had it hard more like.
When he was inducted,
Thrown into Caix.
I want to be pushed
Against the speaker and chilled out.
Time to change the music.

Five thirty-three, realised music had stopped.
End of chill-out mix
First was Penge party
Next I put in Coldplay.
I sense people coming back soon.
I want them to be calm,
And have coke,
And want to smoke weed.
That will help my life
Be calmer,
Following this induction stroke
Sneak copy from inside the Sause.
Muy loco eh!
Something really new and different,
Doesn't even have a street name.
We're on top of it, baby.
From now on it's nothing

But its street-name,
Nothing has a big name like this.
We are onto it,
We're going to get it
To the people
Before it gets banned.
Then there will be no social stigmas
Or Gogman's people
Will take it as a natural part
Of their progressive lives,
Reach mid twenties
Happy with their looks,
Body and mind and soul,
Comfortable life.
Take the sause,
Be happy,
As you are for the rest of your life,
Maybe own an island,
Read a bunch of Playboy,
Or just hangout in the Good Air
Like essentially when they come back.

Five thrity-seven, on the Sause
They should really come back.
With some coke,
And the mind for smoking,
And hanging out,
Maybe looking at some of Josh's art
And being free and young and beautiful.
Being in the graceful periods

Of our lives.
Where all our movements
Look like James Bond's,
Carefully ordered itinerary
Then maybe publish some stuff,
Hang out,
Be really really good looking,
And enjoy the motion of the Good Air,
The motor city,
A place where everybody drives to the club,
Invest in some stuff here,
Get a car to cruise to Pacha,
Everybody drives here,
It's the only way to keep the music flowing.
Here it's nice,
Everybody tunes to the same station,
Ninety-five point One Metrodance.
The city pulsates to one beat.
There is no competition.
Everybody just gets along,
Accepting and relying on the *buena onda,*
The vibe that we share
Beyond all money,
Beyond the sause and the pills,
Or anything really.
We give it to each other as presents,
Something that supports our lives,
Holds large amounts of energy,
To be used by us,
Living mashed off our faces on the Sause.

Five forty-two, still trying to make the spliff,
The music is on a few tracks now.

Five forty-five, realised I stole Ariel's hat.
I am wearing it here in the Sause.
I stole all these things on my way in.
I came in my prime,
Not everyone has the same opportunity.
Look for the Sause early,
While you are still out there.
When you find freedom,
You find the Sause.
You will become one of us.
This is my invitation,
The recording of my search
For this enlightenment,
This transcription on the page,
These words,
In essence a path
Followed to arrive here
In bliss and ecstasy at...

Five forty-seven, trying to break the Sause
To roll a spliff
To get me
To a new plane of thought.
Should get *muy loco,*
Muy loco,
Thinking about how the Sause
Helps people with psychological trauma.

It's helping them see the world as easy,
A place where you can do what you want,
Meditate on it while a make a spliff.

Five forty-nine, still quite fuzzy and fabricky.

Five fifty-one talking to the Sause,
Whispering out-loud.
I need company,
I knew they wouldn't come,
There is no regret.
It's just that I'm ready
To move on
To communicating at
The next level of Sause.

Five fifty-four, *muy loco,*
Multiple personalities
Of Josh and Ariel.
Places of comfort and pleasurability,
Supported by a network of drugs,
A fine balance
We're maintaining,
Pushing the limits of reality
To keep our frail bodies alive.

Five fifty-six, been staring,
Thinking once more
About how funny,
How circular, it all is.

I could go crazy,
End up having to do a bunch of coke,
Or some drawings,
Hang out with a bunch of crazy chicks,
Worry about my serotonin levels

Five fifty-nine, questioning my insanity.

Six o'one, over it all.
The reason of my being has arrived
I am here to give people Sause,
At the right price,
Unveil the hidden fabric world
Of lounges and sofas.
I have the patience.
You will all see.
The patience to bring
All my cool x friends
From Europe
To enjoy the summer,
Trade pills for Sause.
You're all going to love the party
We're going to have.
Sera muy buena fiesta
Eh!

Six o'six,
Spliff O'spliif,
You remind me of the angel dancer,
Emilie of the Moulin Rouge,

Dressed to kill,
Lipstick fire-engine red,
And silver glitter
Dancing to my lips,
Teasing my sexual side
Into taking the smoke
Against my lungs' better will
All under the cover of Sause circularity.

Six o'nine, after a lot of being in awe
Realised that maybe
It is just an over powering drug
Making me be me,
For the first time.
Having travelled around the entire universe
As well as through my own mind,
This little drug
That will die off
In a few hours
Represents the balance of everything
Which always exists
And that now I pay attention to,
All these little details
Flashing through
In a second's impulse
Without delay
Even without the spliff going out.

Six fourteen, going really crazy.

Six nineteen, revelations revolve continuously.
Enlightenment is an infinite tidal wave,
Inundating the shores of our mind,
Continuously,
Forever,
Until the body bears our spirit no longer
And until then all we have
Is to enjoy the fruits given to us,
Right here twisted off our shit on the Sause…

Six thirty-five Elephunk
Feel like I wanna skank somebody
Turnaround and bitch slap somebody

Six forty, enjoying the Sause,
Still mixed up,
Reading through,
Understanding the web inside.
It's all clearing up,
Becoming standard to me,
Second nature already,
Easy to learn and take in,
How to spin out every second.
Moments away
From the clock ticking
On in its continuous ticking
Ad-infinitum.

The circle returns
I cruise down Libertadores,

The radio taxi,
Bumping to...

Ninety-five point One.
Anywhere in the city,
For that matter.
The motor city,
You play some bumped up,
Remixed Cure house trance driving music,
Wind down the window,
Crank it the fuck up,
And watch the city get down,
Until it blows up,
Strobe lights will light up all over,
Glitz the place up,
The bitches start rubbing themselves,
Getting all sweaty and juicy,
Trashing around in the back of the Golf,
Living the shit up here.
Man, make them bitches on the sly!

Six forty-five, marketing mental note
Sausse has a double 's.'
They represent two dragons,
Signifying something really deep
That you will understand
Only when taking the Sausse,
Or by studying linguistics.
No matter how it's spelt
It will have two dragons.

The fiery side of comfortable living…
Sausse is velvet.

Six fifty, realised I am here
To push this drug to the world.
Born to push this
Until it is all over the entire globe,
A one time mind liberator,
A reset button,
A few hours of your life repeating,
Of things making entire sense,
To undo the years of brain-washing.
And now it makes sense to make Sausse.
Jesus probably took Sausse
That time Massive Attack played.
That would make sense.

Six fifty-six, all is making sense
Josh could play the silent partner
I can peddle to Ariel and Eliseo.
Pump out fifteen or twenty a week,
In bundles of five.
Make my dough,
Get in, get out.
Easy.
No lights.
No cameras.
Just living in the Good Air.
Sell it as the one time happy pill.
The only one you'll ever need.

Make my living a while here.
By then it will blow up all over the world,
And I'll have the niche,
In the Latin American market.
Be the insider,
The original peddler
Plot underhand free-trade agreements,
With the mobs of Russia and China,
Steam on through life
In a little guilt free luxury.

Seven o'one, revolutionise the world
With this drug,
Sell the book
As a dummies guide to Sausse.
They buy the book,
Get the pill included in the cover price,
Actually insert it into a capsule,
Lodged inside the back cover.
Sit at home,
Enjoy the experience with this manual.

Seven o'three, accepting that
There is definitely something
Fucking with my brain.
Let's take the people
Back to the pleasure of world's words,
Verbs that caress you.
Nouns that lick your ass out
In the shower,

Suasse words.

Seven ten, the sause formula is complete.
The Scarface fantasy,
You have to feel loved,
Very *especial*
And with a good vibe
To take the Sause,
Get close,
Feel you deserve the Sausse,
Let it work for you,
Let it take you on that journey,
Through the questioning
Of 'Am I important?'
Let it balance everything,
And quell every last doubt
In your mind.
Every decision you've ever taken
Will be explained to you,
A weight will be lifted from your mind,
You will be resolute
On having made the right decision
At every step of the way.
The sause is very circular

Seven twenty-four, the Euros are bad shit.
They're pure bricked up heroin.
Not noticed how nobody is budging on price
Since they came in?
Before Euros arrived,

You could get pills for twenty or twenty five
From a nice guy,
Now even nice guys
Are pushing back to thirty.
People are craving for the horse.
It's why we have been sick.
I think that I am through with it.
I think the Sausse helped me
Realise the problem I had.
Five days in bed,
Loved up and euphoric all the time
Just like all of us.
Destroying the Good Air.
We need to clean up,
Get back to our little capsules,
And to the Sausse of all things

Seven fifty-two *todavía re loco*
Pero hablando en cosas grandes
De ser el rey del Sausse.
¡Ojo!
Very *especial persona*
Re linda persona
I am a writer.
I've written a book about Sausse.
Who should sell it?
This fantasy drug?
Live your dreams
In a dream.

Seven fifty-six,
Josh should be coming soon,
He's gonna be a like
It's fuckin' cold in here,
Then he'll see
I've been taking Sausse,
And he'll get all excited
An start jumpin' on shit,
Pretendin' to break shit.

Seven fifty-nine, ready to rule the world
But still waiting on it arriving.
The Sausse seems slow
To stop revealing sights
Set in time past.
The idea is born,
A book and a drug,
Cut out the coupon on the last page,
Fill it in and post it,
The price of the drug
Is in the price of the book.
We send you the drug free.
You enjoy
A book and a drug.
Read and join the higher frequency
La *buena onda*!

Eight twelve, Sausse is out.

www.ingramcontent.com/pod-product-compliance
Lightning Source LLC
Chambersburg PA
CBHW061324040426
42444CB00011B/2774